The Wombat

THE JOURNAL

.. OF ..

The Geelong Field Naturalists' Club,

.. AND ..

The Gordon College Amateur Photographic Association.

Vols. I to IV.

From August 1895, to July 1899.

NOTE.—The Wombat did not appear in 1900; the Fifth Volume begins November, 1901.

Geelong:
HENRY FRANKS & Co., PRINTERS, MALOP STREET.

1902.

INDEX.

No. 14.

THE WOMBAT.

THE OFFICIAL ORGAN OF THE COLLEGE.

GEO. R. KING, Secretary.

Vol. IV.—No. 2.   **February, 1899.**

THE WOMBAT

(With which is incorporated the *Geelong Naturalist*)

PUBLISHED BY

The Geelong Field Naturalists' & Science Club

AND

The Gordon College Amateur Photographic
Association.

VOL. V, No. 1.　　*January*, 1902.　　No. 17.

*All communications to be addressed to the Editor, Mr. H. E.
Hill, Gordon Technical College, Geelong, Victoria, Australia.*

It is requested that publications sent in exchange may be
addressed to the Editor of the *Wombat.*

The Editor is not responsible for the statements in any paper.

NOTE.

FOR over two years we have been unable to publish, owing to
financial difficulties, but these have fortunately been overcome.
Our last number was dated July 1899, and in it we recorded the
fact that the Gordon College Science Club had amalgamated
with the Geelong Field Naturalists' Club. The name chosen
for the combined society was the Geelong Field Naturalists'
and Science Club, and it holds its meetings on every alternate
Tuesday at the Gordon Technical College.

With this number is published an index to the first four
volumes of the *Wombat*, and with the next number which will be
due in   , will be published an index to the (six volumes of
the) *Geelong Naturalist*, which is now incorporated with the
Wombat.

The proceedings of the A.P.A. are held over till the next
issue.

In an article in *Photography*, with regard to the formation
of a Photographic Society at Blackburn the following remarks
occur ;—" We are sorry to note, however, that it was thought ad-
visable to carry a resolution to the effect that no professional or

THE GORDON COLLEGE PHOTOGRAPHIC CLUB.

SUMMARY OF MEETINGS.

26/7/01. Business and Competition.

The competition rules were altered to the following :—

1. All rules relating to past competitions are rescinded.

2. All pictures shall have been taken since 1/1/01, and no picture shall have been exhibited previously.

3. One judge shall be appointed at the monthly meeting before each competition, and prints shall be in the hands of the secretary on the Wednesday preceding the competition : the secretary shall hand them to the judge, who will furnish a report for the benefit of members.

4. Judging shall be by points—30 for composition, 10 for negative making, 10 for printing and toning, and 3 for mounting.

5. The club's gold medal shall be given for the highest points gained on the year's work under the next rule. (A silver medal is presented by the secretary as a second prize.)

6. In each competition points shall be—3 for first, 2 for second, and one for third ; and there shall be at least three competitors or no second, and four or no third. Points to be counted on one picture only by a single individual in each competition.

7. Should a tie occur in the places for medals, the committee shall select a subject for a further competition to determine the winner.

The competitions in 1900-1 resulted in a tie between Messrs. Creer and Mockridge. As there had been no rule for deciding a tie, it was left to the two members concerned to arrange.

2/8/01. Annual Meeting.

Mr. J. H. Harvey made some remarks on the slides sent to him to judge, and gave the result thus :—J. Wadelton 1, R. B. Mockridge 2, and J. H. M‘Phillimy 3.

The monthly competition resulted thus :—Bromide Groups : R. B. Mockridge 1, D. S. Lord and R. B. Mockridge equal 2.

The report and balance-sheet were presented, the latter showing receipts of £10 17s. 6d., against expenses £35 3s. 3½d.

The election of office-bearers for 1901-2 resulted thus:—
President, H. G. Roebuck.
Vice-presidents, J. Smith and T. Lord.
Question-box editor, J. F. Dentry.
Librarian, F. Price. Assistant, H. Potter.
Press correspondents: W. Westacott and H. Hickson.
Entertainment committee: R. B. Mockridge, G. R. King,
    J. F. Dentry, R. C. Hocking, J. Wadelton and F.
    Price.
Lantern committee: J. Smith, T. Lord, G. H. Brinsmead,
    R. B. Mockridge and F. Price, with power to add.
General committee: W. Thacker, F. Price, J. H.
    M'Phillimy, R. B. Mockridge and G. H. Brinsmead.
Anditors, J. H. M'Phillimy and W. Thacker.
Representatives on *Wombat* Committee, J. Smith and R. B.
    Mockridge.
Treasurer, S. R. J. Mawson.
Secretary, J. Hammerton. Assistant, H. Potter.
9/8/01. Lantern Practice.
16/8/01. }
23/8/01. } Carbon Work. Demonstrations and Practice.
28/8/01. }
30/8/01. Messrs. T. A. Dickson and T. Forrest elected members.
    Competition :—Flower Study : G. H. Brinsmead 1, J. H.
    M'Phillimy 2, W. Roberts 3.
    During August Mr. R. B. Mockridge gave a demonstration
    of Carbon Printing.
6/9/01. Toning. Demonstration.
13/9/01. Public Lantern Lecture, " Ornithology in Southern Aus-
    tralia," by D. Le Souëf, C.M.Z.S. This was held in
    conjunction with the Field Naturalists' Club.
20/9/01. Mr. Slocum, of the Kodak Company, gave a demonstra-
    tion of the development of films.
27/9/01. Business Meeting. Mr. R. Wilson elected a member.
    Competition :—Child Study : H. Potter 1, 2 and 3.
4/10/01. Enlarging Evening. Practice.
11/10/01. Public Lecture, " The Discovery of Gold," by Mr. Jas.
    Oddie. In conjunction with the F.N.C.
18/10/01. Demonstration. Carbon work; double transfer. Mr.
    J. H. Harvey.
25/10/01. Business Meeting.
    Competition:—Moonlight Effect: J. Wadelton and R.
    Mockridge equal, H. Potter 3.
1/11/01. Lantern Slide Making and Reducing. Mr. G. H.
    Brinsmead.
5/11/01. Complimentary Social to Mr. J. B. Leitch. In conjunc-
    with the F.N.C.
8/11/01. Enamelling P.O.P. Mr. A. E. Bratley.
11/11/01. King's Birthday. Excursion to Sheoak Falls, Moora-
    bool River. A successful trip, about thirty joining in

22/11/01. Business Meeting. The secretary reported having had a visit from Mr. Darling, of the Deniliquin Club, but he was unfortunately not able to stay for our meeting.

Competition :—Landscape ; P.O.P. Enamelled : D. Lord 1, J. H. M'Phillimy 2 and 3.

King's Birthday Pictures :—Landscape, Mr Brinsmead's trophy : D. Lord 1, J. H. M'Phillimy 2 and 3. Group, Mr. Hammerton's trophy : J. H. M'Phillimy. Tableau, Mr King's trophy : W. Thacker.

29/11/01. Toning Bromides. Mr. H. Potter.

6/12/01. Business and Competition. Enlargement :—Landscape·

13/12/01. Concert. Last meeting for the year.

THE GEELONG FIELD NATURALISTS' CLUB. ·

SUMMARY OF MEETINGS.

11/10/01. Lecture on the Discovery of Gold. Mr. Jas. Oddie· In conjunction with the A.P.A.

22/10/01. Exhibition of Specimens.

5/11/01. Social to Mr. J. B. Leitch to welcome him on his return from South Africa. In conjunction with the A.P.A.

19/11/01. Paper, "The Irritability of Plants. Mr. G. H. Adcock, F.L.S.

3/12/01. Paper, "Reflections on the Discovery of the Batman Deeds. Mr. J. J. Cary. Illustrated by photographic copies of the deeds.

A considerable donation of books for the library was received from Mr. G. H. Adcock, F.L.S.

17/12/01. Magazine Night.

The following publications were received during the quarter :— *Victorian Naturalist*, Vol. XVIII., Nos. 6, 7 and 8, *Proc. Roy. Geog. Soc.*, Vict. Branch, Vol. XIX., *The Zoologist*, Nos. 723-4, Pamphlets from the Yorkshire Naturalists' Union ; and U.S. Geol. Surv., VIII. Ann. Rpt. Part 2, Geikie's *Outlines of Field Geology*, Geikie's *Classbook of Geology*, Page's *Text-book of Geology*, *Experimental Mechanics*, Heath's *Fern Paradise*, Landsborough's *Popular History of British Zoophytes*, Lacoppidan's *Agricultural Teacher*.

Hot Hypo-alum Toning for Bromide Prints. For this method of toning it is not necessary that the prints should be washed after fixing—a mere rinse will be quite sufficient—but I think it is better that they should be dried before attempting to tone them, as this tends to harden the gelatine.

Before placing the prints in the hot hypo-alum bath, they must either be put in an alum bath or placed in a cold hypo and alum bath for a few minutes, and then transferred to the hot bath, which is made up as follows :—

Sodium hyposulphite	...	...	9 oz.
Alum (common)	...	...	1 oz.
Water	...	...	60 oz.

This bath requires to be heated to about 120° before the prints are put in, and then kept to about that temperature. The prints take from twenty to forty minutes to tone. The quality of the tones obtained by this process depends mainly upon the quality of the print. Prints taken from brilliant negatives give very fine tones indeed. The best paper for this purpose is a toned or tinted one, such as Eastman's Royal Bromide, and some very fine effects indeed may be obtained on this paper, almost approaching carbon in quality. It must be remembered that this method of toning tends to slightly reduce the prints, and therefore the prints for this purpose must be fully printed out.—*Photography*.

SOME OF THE DEFECTS IN PLATINOTYPE WORK AND THEIR CAUSES.

1. The pictures are vigorous, but more or less fogged.
    Cause.—The paper was affected by light, either in sensitising or copying, or there was too high a temperature in drying; it should not exceed 40° C.
    Spoiled ferric solution.
    The ferric solution is best preserved in hyalite flasks. If you are not sure of your solution, test it before using with red prussiate of potash to see that it is free from ferrite. Should it contain only a trace of ferrite, it can be made fit for use again by carefully adding red prussiate of potash. In order to try this, mix a few cub. centims. of the norms-ferric-chlorite solution with every 100 cub. centims of the iron solution, and ascertain by actual experiment on paper whether the restoration is complete.

2. The prints appear weak under the developer.
    Paper which has become damp.

3. The prints come out vigorously in developing, but become weak
   after being dried.
   Paper not sufficiently sized, for which reason the images sink
       into its substance, or the drying of the paper has been too
       slow.
4. The whites of the prints have, after drying, a more 'or less
   yellowish tinge.
   The sensitising solution in the developer is not sufficiently
       acid, or there has been insufficient immersion in hydrochloric
       acid.
5. Black spots.
   Particles of metal embedded in the substance of the paper,
       causing a reduction of the platinum.
   May be due also to insoluble impurities in the chloro-platinite
       of potassium.
   These spots have a black nucleus with an extension of lighter
       colour, like the tail of a comet.

A FEW DEFECTS IN THE SEPIA PAPER SOLD BY THE PLATINOTYPE COMPANY.

A dirty, yellowish veil appearing on development all over the print, but more observable in the lighter portions, is due to one of the following causes :—1. Want of sufficient "Special Solution" in the developer. 2. Too much exposure of the developing solution to light. 3. Use of a dish in which the enamel is cracked so as to expose the iron.—*(Compiled)* J.B.L.

A LIST OF COLEOPTERA COLLECTED NEAR GEELONG.

By J. F. Mulder.

PART I.—Family *Carabidæ*.

34.	*Calosoma schayeri* (Er.)	Found in the hayfields in summertime, Geelong.
118.	*Xanthophœa grandis* (Chaud.)	Under bark of gum-trees, Geelong.
127.	„ *vittata* (Dej.)	Geelong.
	„ *brachinoderus* (Chaud,)	Under bark of gum-trees, Princes Bridge, Geelong.

139. *Dromius crudelis* (Newm.)	Geelong.
,, *notophiloides* (Sloane)	,,
,, *australiensis* (Sloane)	,,
,, *yarraensis* (Blackb.)	,,
Sarothrocrepis d'urvilli (Blanch.)	,, .
160. *Philophlæus australis* (Dej)	,,
164. ,, *eucalypti* (Germ.)	,,
170. ,, *luculentus* (Newm,)	,,
Agonochila (sp.)	,,
Silphomorpha (2 sp.)	,,
404. *Carenum scaritoides* (Westw.)	Under stones, Marnock Vale.
,, *loculosum* (Newm.)	Under stones, Marnock Vale.
451. *Scaraphites insulans* (Sloane)	A large and powerful insect was collected for me by Mr. J. Davis, of Bellarine; he brought me several specimens, and said that they were fairly plentiful in the potato fields.
501. *Olivina australasiæ* (Bohem.)	Under logs and rubbish Barwon River.
,, *planiceps* (Putz.)	Under logs and rubbish, Barwon River.
532. *Epicosmus australasiæ*	Geelong.
585. *Promecoderus brunnicornis* (Dej.)	Under cowdung and rubbish, Highton.
598. ,, *lucidicollis* (Cart.)	Under cowdung and rubbish, Highton.
Percosoma montana (Casteln.)	Geelong.
675. *Hypharpax australis* (Dej)	In garden at Highton.
675. ,, *inornatus* (Germ.)	,, ,, ,, ,,
,, sp. (allied to *H. æreus* Dej.) Geelong.	
683. *Diaphoromerus germari* (Casteln.)	,,
Thenarotes atriceps (Meul.)	,,
7470. *Notophilus parius* (Blackb.)	Bank of Barwon.
727. *Cyclothorax ambiguus* (Er.)	In garden at Highton.
731. *Stenolophus dingo* (Casteln.)	Geelong.
Amblytelus brevis (Blackb.)	Under gum bark, Geelong.
758. *Catadtomus lacardairii* (Bois.)	Geelong.
823. *Notonomus philippi* (Newm.)	Under logs, Cape Otway Ranges and Geelong.
Notonomus (3 species)	Cape Otway Ranges.

for Section F, of which I was Secretary. This he accordingly did.
The paper was read at one of the meetings of the Section, and was
handed to a small committee of three members for further
consideration. I do not know if that committee made any use of
Mr. Cary's communication or reported on it, but the paper itself
was published in Vol. VII. (Sydney meeting) of the *Australasian
Association for the Advancement of Science*. Since then, I have
given a little more careful attention to these Woddowro pronouns,
and, in consequence, I seem to understand what they are. The
results of my investigation I am now requested to make known in
the pages of the *Wombat*. Mr. Cary's discovery is unique and
important, for the Australian dialects have not furnished any other
instance of the use of a *ternal* number in the pronouns, and this
example of it serves as a link to connect our blacks with the
Melanesians of the islands of the Western Pacific.

The history of the discovery is this. In the year 1838—only
a few years later that the first settlement of white men on the
shores of Port Phillip—the Wesleyan Methodists began a mission
to the Woddowro, Dautgurt and Kolijon tribes, in what is now the
Geelong district. One of those who engaged in this labour of love
was Francis Tuckfield, a young man who had come from Cornwall,
full of hope and zeal for the betterment of the natives by trying to
christianize and civilize them. In this work he spent ten of the
best years of his life. Mr. Cary goes on to say, " A large
vocabulary was compiled in the first years of the mission, but it was
unfortunately lost in a fire that destroyed the mission-house.
. . . . In his note book is preserved a collection of about two
hundred short sentences, some translations of Scripture, and a
vocabulary of over two hundred words. By the kindness of the
Tuckfield family, it has been my privilege to inspect their father's
journal, letters, and note book ; and, when perusing the latter, I
unearthed a grammatical form of number hitherto practically
unnoticed as a peculiarity in Australian language. That dual
number is a feature of several Australian dialects is well-known ;
but with the Woddowro, number as a means of precision was
amplified yet another degree. And herein lies the discovery ;
these natives of the Geelong district used triple number."

This then is the history of the case ; I will now proceed to
show what I can make of it. And in doing so, I shall use the
terms Singular, Binal, Ternal, Plural number. The word ' dual '
has so established itself in grammar that everybody seems to have
acquiesced in its use, but, on the analogy of Singular
(from Lat. *singuli*, ' one-by-one ') it ought to be Binal,
which is suitable, for it marks that two are spoken of *each time*.
The name ' trial ' for the triple number is an awkward word ; and
so, on analogy again, I use Ternal. And in discussing this
question I will advance by a series of Propositions.

Humble & Sons,

(Late HUMBLE & NICHOLSON)

Vulcan Foundry, Geelong

Engineers, Boiler Makers, Shipwrights, Iron and Brass Founders.

Manufacturers of 

REFRIGERATING MACHINERY for Butter, Bacon and Ice
Factories, Butchers, Hotels and cold storage of all perishable
products.

STEAM, GAS AND OIL ENGINES.

STEAM BOILERS—Cornish, Multitubular, Lancashire,
Vertical, &c., for every description of work.

WOOL PRESSES.

CONTINUOUS HAY-BALING MACHINERY.

HYDRAULIC PRESSES AND LIFTS.

ROPE-MAKING, TANNERS, AND WOOL WASHING
MACHINERY.

HORSEWORKS.

THRASHERS AND WINNOWERS.

RAILWAY CONTRACTORS' PLANT.

RABBIT POISON DISTRIBUTORS, FOR POLLARD OR
GRAIN.

WATER TANKS.

CRAB WINCHES.

PUMPS.

BUILDERS' IRONWORK OF ALL DESCRIPTIONS, &c.

THE WOMBAT

(And *Geelong Naturalist.*)

PUBLISHED BY

The Geelong Field Naturalists' Club

AND

The Gordon College Photographic Club.

VOL. V, No. 4.   *December,* 1902.   No. 20

It is requested that all publications and exchanges be addressed to the Editor, at the Gordon Technical College, Geelong, Victoria, Australia.

Correspondence should be addressed to the Hon. Sec. of the Field Naturalists' Club or Photographic Club as the case may be.

THE GEELONG FIELD NATURALISTS' CLUB.

Meetings have been held during the half-year as under :—

4TH JULY.—Mr. J. C. Taylor gave a Lecturette illustrative of a voyage through the South Pacific Islands. Specimens of the natural products and native industries of the Islands were exhibited, and a very large number of excellent lantern views shown.

1ST AUGUST.—A paper on Foraminifera by Mr. Bartlett was in his absence read by Mr. J. F. Mulder. The paper was illustrated by microscopic slides.

5TH SEPT.—Mr. J. F. Denny read a paper describing the existing Chemical Process of Extracting Gold. Models which well explained the methods of gold extraction dealt

with had been constructed by the lecturer especially for the occasion, and proved of great service in making an intricate subject clear.

3RD OCTOBER.—The President (Mr. G. H. Adcock) read a very interesting paper "On a recently-identified Australian Fungus (*Armillaria mellea, Vahl*)." Mr. Adcock after some years' close watching detected this harmful parasitic growth on trees at Rutherglen in the North East, and obtained there the specimens which he brought to illustrate his paper. At its conclusion, many questions were asked by members as to the best modes of dealing with fungus growths in fruit trees, and the President gave some valuable information in reply.

7TH NOVEMBER.—The Rev. R. C. Nugent Kelly gave the Club a Lecturette on "The Old Fish Camps of the Tasmanian Blacks." Several of the crude implements with which the aborigines of that long extinct race used to extract the shell-fish from their shells, and also their flesh-scrapers and rough axeheads were laid upon the Club's table. A great deal of discussion relative to the Tasmanian and Mainland Blacks and their habits followed, and members felt indebted to Mr. Kelly for a very instructive evening.

5TH DECEMBER.—Mr. J. J. Cary read a paper on "The Place-names of the Geelong District." The subject was dealt with chiefly from the historical standpoint, but the probable meanings of the local native names were also considered. The lecturer drew attention to the variations, eleven in all, through which the word Corio passed before reaching its now familiar form. Many interesting reminiscences of the thirties and forties were alluded to.

Each of the foregoing papers and lectures was preceded by the usual business meeting. The average attendance has been highly satisfactory, considering the smallness of our numbers, and is increasing, thanks to the efforts of the Hon. Sec., Mr. A. B. F. Wilson.

THE GORDON COLLEGE PHOTOGRAPHIC CLUB.

SINCE our last issue the Club has made good progress. Several new members have joined and a lot of good work has been done. There has been considerable improvement shown in the work sent in for competition by the younger members of the Club, who have done especially well in the artistic composition of their pictures, and as it is for this that most marks are awarded, they have gained many places in the competitions.

The officers of the Club desire to thank those gentlemen who from time to time have come from Melbourne and given practical demonstrations for the Club's benefit, especially Messrs. R. Harvie and J. H. Harvey (Melbourne Kodak Co). Lantern slide reducing, Enlargements, Velox Paper, "Photo Dodges," Carbon Work, Architectural Studies, Bird Life Studies, Landscape with Figures, Groups, Instantaneous work, and other interesting branches of Photographic work have been undertaken with good results. Anything of novelty has been eagerly taken up, and the Club has been fortunate in receiving samples, booklets and journals from Photographic firms which are always welcome and thoroughly discussed.

The Club outing took place on 10th November. Anglesea River was the chosen spot. Leaving the College at 6.15 a.m., thirty-five members and friends had a long and enjoyable day. Arrived at the River, boats were soon manned, and the beauty spots explored for pictorial "game." Prizes were offered for the best work in group, landscape (with and without figures), and instantaneous work respectively. A high level was reached by many competitors, and the judges had no easy task. Mr. S. R. J. Mawson kindly opened his grounds to the Club, and the shelter was much appreciated.

The last meeting for the year was held on 12th December. The attendance was large. After the usual business, the pictures taken at Anglesea were exhibited and favourably criticised. The Syllabus for the first half of 1903 was settled, and the following subjects selected for the monthly competitions :— Yachting, Street Scenes, Animals, Architectural Work, Enlargements, Landscape, River or Lake Views, and Plate Development. Messrs. W. Wrathall, W. Thacker and T. Lord have offered special prizes. Not fewer than six may compete in each section. Competitors for the Plate Development Prize must each bring the exposed plate to the meeting, with particulars of time, make, and his "nom-de-plume." The plates are numbered and drawn for by lot; each competitor developes the plate he draws, using any developer he pleases. The negatives will then be judged, and finally the names of the competitors will be made known.

It is intended early in the New Year to fit up a daylight enlarging camera for the use of members.

The Club's Dark Room is always at the disposal of visitors to Geelong, and the Hon Secretary is happy to afford all information that may be wished. The Club would be thankful if firms who issue photographic publications or Lists would forward copies of same to the Hon. Sec., Mr. J. Hammerton, jun.

SOUTHWARDS.

A THREE days' holiday at the end of September presented what seemed a good opportunity for extending our acquaintance with the birds of the Southern woodlands, and so the close of a grey Spring afternoon found us wheeling along the road to Anglesea River. Some seven miles out we skirted a small plantation of black wattles and could hear the Little Tits (*Acanthiza nana*) chirping lightly from the foliage. Wattle plantations in otherwise fairly open country are this bird's chief resort, whilst its allies *A. pusilla* and *A. lineata* prefer respectively the ti-tree thickets and forests of messmate. At Freshwater Creek we heard a Pardalote by the creek side : no doubt it was *P. assimilis*, which is the common species with us.

From this point we had two or three miles of grasstree plain patched with honeysuckle to traverse. The Fulvous-fronted Honeyeater (*Glycyphila fulvifrons*) showed itself once or twice piping weirdly from the wayside shrubs. Nearer Jan Juc a clump of mimosa in flower among the honeysuckes looked promising, and going over to inspect, I was rewarded with a sight of the White-face (*Xerophila leucopsis*). I got close enough to make absolutely sure of the bird, which I have now noted three times in as many places along the same road this Spring. Many Scarlet-breasted Robins (*Petroeca leggii*) flitted between the stunted trees, and in a mimosa bush a nest which I took took to be that of the Tomtit (*Geobasileus chrysorrhoa*) yielded a single egg of the Narrow-billed Bronze Cuckoo (*Lamprococcyx basalis*). The shadows lengthened and my companions were thinking of the long forest road in front, so I rejoined them and we sped down the hillside to the village, to wind up the steep southern ascent. One comes into the bush suddenly at the top of this hill ; the messmate forest with that subtle delicate aroma of gum leaves and wholesome earth of the wilderness which is so swift to recall the associations of boyhood. First of the bush birds we saw the Buff-rumped Tit (*G. reguloides*) which is plentiful hence right down to the coast. This species represents the Tomtit of the more open country and is so close to the latter bird respect of its colouration, song and general habits that I think it better classed with the Tomtit under the genus *Geobasileus* and separated from the *Acanthizae*. Its only close resemblance to the *Acanthizae* is in its nidification : the nest is smaller and a great deal more compact than the Tomtits', and is placed either on the ground at the foot of a tuft of bush herbage, or (more usually in this forest) in a recess in the bark of a large tree. Otherwise it appears to be descended almost recently from a common ancestor with the Tomtit : each form being modified therefrom to suit its particular environment. Note the quieter colours and soberer song of the Buff-rumped Tit, and compare it in these respects with the bright little bird of the sunlit roadside hedges that sings as Gould noted so like the English Goldfinch.

The Scarlet-breasted Robins and Brown Flycatchers (*Micrœca fascinans*) were at first numerous, but became scarcer as we proceeded further into the bush, and we heard now the Striated Tits (*A. lineata*) from the topmost messmate twigs, ceaselessly with faint twittering hunting their insect food. Well after dark we pedalled into Anglesea, having got over the 25 miles without mishap. The road had been good all the way, especially the nine unmetalled miles from Jan Juc

Next morning we awoke early to the music of Harmonious Thrushes (*Collyriocincla harmonica*) and White-eared Honeyeaters (*Ptilotis leucotis*), and looking out toward the sea, descried a pair of hawks circling over the marshy ground. I decided upon a swim in the creek, so walked about half a mile along the eastern bank through the ti-tree scrub to the bathing place. On the other side I heard Tasmanian Honeyeaters (*Lichmera Australasiana*), and I also noted the Summer Bird (*Graucalus melanops*), Wattle Bird (*Acanthochœra carunculata*), Short-billed Honeyeater (*Melithreptus brevirostris*) and a Pardalote : but there was not much variety of species, and I felt disappointed. Welcome Swallows (*Hirundo neoxena*) had a nest on a rafter in the boat-house by which I bathed.

The swim over, I left the flat land by the river and struck into the messmate country on the hillside. Here the Striated Tits were very numerous, and a Parrakeet, which so far as I could make out was the Orange-bellied (*Euphema chrysogastra*), flew from a tree near me and away to a distant hill. An open heath of twenty or thirty acres, carpeted with blue and yellow flowers, was the home of many Fulvous-fronted Honeyeaters, and in a gully to the south a pair of Chocolate Birds (*Chthonicola sagittata*) got up from some coarse grass, but I could not find a nest.

A strong north-west wind sprang up during the morning, making the conditions unfavourable for observation. We kept to the scrubby country, and after patiently watching a pair of Brown

Tits (*A. pusilla*) for some time, saw one of them fly down to a patch of bracken, where their nest was beautifully built in the dead curled top of a fern. It contained three newly hatched young.

W. had to return to Geelong that evening, so A. and I parted from him to continue our ride to Airey's Inlet, eight miles to the westward. The road lies through messmate and peppermint scrub all the way, and rises steeply at first till the top of "Mount Misery" is reached. The wind had veered into the west and brought with it driving showers of rain, through which, as we reached the flat top of the hill, we saw on our right the bare desolate country dipping to the Anglesea Valley and rising again on the north towards the upland plains about Mount Moriac. A solitary Eagle (*Aquila audax*) sailed majestically athwart the valley. The cry of a Grey Crow-shrike (*Strepera fuliginosa*) sounded close at hand; we left the track and crossed the heath to see if it were nesting in some dwarf gums, but without success. Returning, I was startled by a bird that flew hurriedly from almost under my feet. It was a Fulvous-fronted Honey-eater, and in the nest, cunningly placed a few inches from the ground in a small heath-like plant, were a pair of white eggs sparingly spotted with brownish red at the larger end. I wondered no longer that I had never previously found this bird's eggs. It would only be possible to discover the nest by some such chance as this, or else by a systematic beating of the ground at dusk.

We presently reached a spot known as the Hut Gully, where a small creek crosses the road and there is a thicket of ti-tree. This held three nests of the Brown Tit, of which one belonged to last season, one had been used earlier in this, and the third contained three half-fledged young. All the nests were about five feet from the ground. Right on the road in the same thicket, was an empty nest of the Tasmanian Honeyeater. The birds were about and the nest seemed new.

A mile further on is a flat timbered with the graceful peppermint gums. Here a bevy of Choughs (*Corcorax melanorhamphus*) were conspicuous with black and white plumage as they flew from tree to tree, alternately whistling mournfully and screeching. From a tall messmate over the road a Grey Crow-shrike slipped silently. Standing beneath, we saw the nest far out on one of the top boughs, but the tree was high and the sunset near, so we deferred consideration of the matter till our return.

Hence to Airey's the road follows the Distil Creek, at a distance of a hundred yards or so all the way, and from the scrubby banks we heard several species of Honeyeaters calling, while all the other bush birds seemed to increase in numbers. Presently we crossed the Distil and Alum Creeks, which unite a little further down and form Airey's Creek. The timber is taller in this part, with the stately ironbark rising above the messmate. By six o'clock we had arrived at our destination.

We were up betimes to greet a glorious morning, and strolled before breakfast among the mimosa bushes by the creek. The New Holland Honeyeaters (*Meliornis Novæ Hollandiæ*) were everywhere, and we found numbers of their nests, mostly finished with, as this species breeds early. One or two contained clutches of hard-set eggs. A Magpie Lark (*Grallina picata*) sat on her mud-bowl on a gum branch hanging over the river, and about her flew a Restless Flycatcher (*Seisura inquieta*) with noises like the grinding of scissors. I have observed that with the advance of civilization this bird has taken the place of the Shining Flycatcher (*Myiagra nitida*) which used to be common at Airey's Inlet, but has now gone farther back up the creeks, while the Restless Flycatcher has come in with the Rosella, the Mina, and other birds of the open.

About ten o'clock we set out for a spot about a mile away along the course of the creek, where we knew we should find swamps with very dense mimosa thickets in the vicinity. On the way we met with a nest of the White-fronted Sericornis (*S. frontalis*) with three young able to fly. Though the nest was in an open patch between ferns, we should never found it but for the bird, so thoroughly had it been brought into harmony with its surroundings. This is characteristic of the Sericornes, which do not build a neat nest, but attain the security they need by assimilating it in contour and material to the position in which it is placed.

At intervals along the track were small swampy flats, where ti-tree and mimosa grew: in these we searched for the nest of the Tasmanian Honeyeater, finding one at last from which the young had just flown. We concluded that this bird, like the New Holland Honeyeater, bred chiefly in August and early September.

The spot we were making for was where the telegraph line from Lorne to Winchelsea crosses Airey's Creek. There is here an extensive flat from which a good deal of the higher timber has been cleared, leaving free scope for the ironbark scrub and mimosa to spread, while on the banks of the creek itself and along the swamps which run parallel with it are dense growths of ti-tree and a species of light scrub called "shortwood" locally. Most of the scrub was in flower, yellow or white, and the various kinds of Honeyeaters appeared to be holding a sort of harvest festival. One could easily imagine it was the original home from which the tribe of Meliphagidae had spread down the creeks and gullies of all the Eastern Otway. The air resounded with the bark of Wattle birds (*Acanthochaera carunculata*) and their smaller brush brethren (*Anellobia mellivora*), while everywhere we heard we heard

the not unmusical staccato of the Tasmanian Honeyeater. Numerically the New Holland Honeyeaters were strongest, their nests were found at every turn, fixed firmly in the forks of mimosa bushes.

A nest set low down in ferns caught my companion's eye; it held three eggs rather small for the New Holland Honeyeater, so he called me over. I diagnosed Tasmanian Honeyeater, and waited to see. The New Holland birds flew about our heads as we lay concealed, but did not go to the nest, on to which presently crept a female Tasmanian Honeyeater. Thus sure of the bird, we examined the nest closely to see wherein it differed from that of its near cousin. In the first place it was a good deal broader. Between the outside frame of light twigs and the lining were three or four large dried leaves. The lining itself was of fine grass, as contrasted with that of the New Holland Honeyeater's which is in nine cases out of ten composed of one kind or another of seed down. We examined several nests of this species subsequently and always found these distinguishing marks. Besides, the eggs are a good deal smaller as a rule, though I think I have seen one or two New Holland Honeyeater's eggs not much larger than the Tasmanian's that we found.

A. penetrated a belt of shortwood scrub, and had the good fortune to discover within a few yards of each other two nests of the Brush Wattle Bird, each with a pair of eggs, one clutch being of the dark and the other of the light type. The nests were built about 10 feet from the ground in shortwoods about 15 or 20 feet high, and appeared very small for the size of the bird. In this respect they are like the Spiny Cheeked Honeyeater's nests, but are flattish structures, lined with bark and grass and built in a fork, and so easily distinguishable from those of the latter bird which are pensile and well woven. The eggs of the two species present more similarity than the nests, but the advantage in point of size is clearly with the Brush Wattle Bird.

Close to the edge of a swamp a pair of White-fronted Sericornes had a nest with feathered young. In this case the position chosen was in a mass of tangled vegetation about three feet from the ground.

I flushed a Bronzewing Pigeon from a meal of ironbark scrub seeds, a favourite food of this bird. Other birds we noted were the Musk Lorikeet (*Glossopsittacus concinnus*) and one of its smaller congeners, probably the Purple-crowned, and also the Red Lory (*Platycercus pennantii*). Those of the latter species we saw had not attained their full plumage. They breed in these forests, but are careful as a rule to select inaccessible spouts in tall gums. We heard however of a nest with eggs found about the middle of the month (September) in the scrub at the back of Anglesea.

Returning by a somewhat different route to Airey's Inlet, we came upon several more nests of the Tasmanian Honeyeater, all built within a couple of feet of the ground. One contained a single addled egg.

The same evening we rode back to Anglesea, halting now and again where birds were plentiful. The tall messmate that held the Crow Shrike's nest we had found the day before tried first the climbing capacity and then the nerve of my young companion to the utmost, but he persevered till leaning far out he reached the coveted prize: a pair of pink-flushed eggs, of which one unfortunately struck a ridge in the hat I held beneath to receive it, and broke.

We spent the night at Anglesea, and left for home after breakfast the following morning. We were tempted to explore a swamp lying in a gully a few miles along the road. There seemed no bird life about at all; but presently the cry of a hawk reached us from above, and looking up we saw the bird, first a speck in the blue vault, and then increasing to the vision, as with swoops and wheelings it flashed downwards to the reedy pool not thirty yards from where we stood. Just as it seemed to touch the reeds and we recognised it as the male Swamp Hawk (*Circus Gouldi*) its larger mate flapped heavily up from beneath. We waded in, but only found a few feathers and some bent down reeds, so that it was evident nest-building proper had not commenced.

Two miles on we met a party of Choughs, and found one of their mud-built nests high up a tall Eucalypt, quite safe from any sort of interference.

Near Jan Juc the Orange-winged Tree Runner (*Sittella chrysoptera*) was noticed, and a Robin's (*P. Leggii*) nest with young. In an adjacent tree a Frontal Shrike-tit, a bird not often seen in these parts, was busy cracking a piece of bark for insects.

A. was very anxious to find the nest of the White-face which I had seen on the outward journey. I did not think much of his chance of finding it, and was therefore considerably surprised when he returned to where I was waiting on the road with a pair of the unmistakable spotted eggs in his hand. He had got them from the nest from which I took the cuckoo's egg three days before, and which I certainly thought was an ordinary tomtit's nest. I went over with him to inspect the nest more closely, but there was absolutely nothing about it by which it could be differentiated from the nest of *G. chrysorrhoa* unless it were a slightly larger entrance, which might very well have been caused by the cuckoo. There were several tomtits about: perhaps they had built the nest, and the Whiteface having observed the Cuckoo's labour-saving device had followed suit.

The only other nest of this bird (which is strictly speaking an interior species), that I have seen in the Geelong district was one built in a sheoak on the plains at the foot of the You Yangs, which contained three fresh eggs. That was late in July, 1896, and I have only noticed the birds four times since, so that the occurrence now recorded is somewhat exceptional. The White-face is hardly likely to be discovered, I think, further to the southward, as the nest was only a bare mile from the edge of the costal ranges, and the bird is a plain-dweller.

A pleasant ride of fifteen miles brought us home early in the afternoon, and so concluded an outing that we are likely to long remember as one in every daylight hour of which we learned something of fresh interest (to ourselves at least) about the birds of our district. Very soon the greater part of this forest will have been cut down for fire-wood; and as the trees go, the birds go too. Within my easy recollection some species were almost common in our district that are never now seen. It is likely that in the generation following us there will be ornithologists who will be glad to know what species existed in this part of the country in the days that preceded them, and it is for such chiefly that I have written this account of this excursion, though I trust I have not made it too long and uninteresting for the present-day reader. I know the birds mentioned in it are common enough now: my excuse for writing about them is that they will not always be.

C.F.B.

FORAMINIFERA.

The following is a list of Foraminifera occurring in the Curlewis and Shelford beds, as identified by Messrs. E. J. Brady and J. F. Mulder. It is hoped that as additional species are brought to light from time to time in the future members interested in this study will supply the particulars necessary to extend the list in later numbers of " The Wombat."

A. Imperforate or Porcellaneous Foraminifera.

    I. MILIOLIDA—

        A. Cornuspira (*Schultze*)

1.	Cornuspira poliacea (*Phil*)	Shelford
2.	,, involvens ,,	Shelford & Curlewis

        B. Miliolina (*Lamarck*)

3.	Miliolina seminulum (*Linne*)	Shelford & Curlewis
4.	,, agglutinans (*D'Orb*)	,, ,,
5.	,, tricarinata ,,	,, ,,
6.	,, cuvieraua ,,	Curlewis
7.	,, circularis (*Bornemann*)	,,
8.	,, linneana (*D'Orb*)	,,
9.	Biloculina depressa ,,	Shelford & Curlewis
10.	,, builoides ,,	,, ,,
11.	,, irregularis ,,	Curlewis
12.	,, ringens (*Lamarck*)	,,
13.	Spiroloculina asperula (*Karrer*)	,,

B. Perforate or Hyaline Foraminifera.

    I. LAGENIDA—

        A. Nodosaria (*Parker & Jones*)

14.	Nodosaria consobrina (*D'Orb*)	Shelford
15.	,, lævigata ,,	,,
16.	,, raphanus (*Linne*)	Curlewis
17.	,, soluta (*Reuss*)	,,
18.	Cristellaria cultrata (*Montfort*)	Shelford & Curlewis
19.	,, crepidula (*F & M*)	Curlewis
20.	,, articulata (*Reuss*)	,,
21.	Marginulina costata (*Batsch*)	,,

II. POLYMORPHINIDA—

    A. Polymorphina

      22. Polymorphina lactea (*W & J*)   Curlewis
                (fistulose variety)
      23.   „   elegantissima (*P & J*)   „

    B. Uvigerina (*D'Orb*)
      24. Uvigerina interrupta (*Brady*)   „

III. BULIMINIDA—

    A. Bulimina (*L'Orb*)

      25. Bulimina elegantissima (*D'Orb*)   Curlewis
      26. Bolivina punctata   „   „

IV. TEXTILARIDA—

    A. Textilaria (*Defrance*)
      27. Textilaria sagittula (*Def.*)   Shelford &
                            Curlewis
      28. Clavulina communis (*D'Orb*)   Curlewis
      29. Quadryina rufosa   „   Shelford

V. GLOBIGERINIDA—

    A. Globigerina
      30. Orbulina universa (*D'Orb*)   Curlewis
      31. Globigerina bulloides „   „
      31A.   „   „ var. triloba (*Reuss*) Shelford
      32.   „   inflata   (*D'Orb*) Curlewis
      32A. Sphæroidina bulloides „   „

    B. Rotalina
        Planorbulina (*D'Orb*)
      33. Truncatulina reticulata (*Czjzek*)   ‘Curlewis
      34.   „   variabilis (*D'Orb*)   „
      35.   „   harderingeri „   „
      36.   „   lobatula (*W & J*)   Shelford

    C. Polystomellina
        Polystomella (*Lamarck*)
      37. Monionina depressula (*W & J*)   Curlewis

    D. Nummicilinina
        Nummicilina (*D'Orb*)

      38. Operculina complanata (*Def.*   Shelford &
                            Curlewis

NOTES.

THE Field Naturalists' Club has during the past half-year met on the first Friday in each month only. This has been found not to afford sufficient time to cope properly with the work to be done, and with the new year fortnightly meetings will be inaugurated.

The Gordon College Museum has been handed over to the control of the Field Club, whose executive have appointed as curator Mr. W. Shaw. Under his careful guidance the museum is re-assuming an appearance of order. The specimens have, to a great extent, been re-grouped, and set out in a more attractive manner than heretofore.

The drought is responsible for the appearance of some rare bird-visitants to Southern Victoria during the past spring. The beautiful Blood Honeyeater (*Myzomela sanguineolenta*) came down from its home in the tropical scrubs of the north and was seen in various localities south of Melbourne. A specimen shot at Queenscliff by Mr. Batchelder was exhibited on September 5th before the club by Mr. W. Shaw. The rich metallic red of the bird's head and neck, and the minuteness of its body (only four inches long altogether), made the skin an object of great interest.

In connection with the list of shells from King Island, which appeared in our last issue, it should have been stated that about half the species enumerated had previously been noted from Victoria, and not from Tasmania, while the other half consisted of purely Tasmanian forms. This is interesting as another proof of the connection that once existed between Tasmania and the mainland.

The Game Act has been amended so as to extend the close season for ducks from the 21st December to the 31st January, so that the birds will have henceforth a clear half-year's rest from the 1st August onwards. All bird-lovers will agree that the alteration is a wise one. It may be hard upon those sportsmen whose only chance for shooting is the Christmas vacation, but it will put a stop to the slaughter of "flappers" that has hitherto occurred annually in certain parts of the State at the opening of the season, and so give the birds a chance to increase.

Another significant alteration of the Act concerns imported birds. Formerly all birds not indigenous to Australia, except Sparrows and (Indian) Minahs, were protected throughout the year.

For the future only the English Thrush and Skylark, and the Java Dove, are to enjoy this immunity. That is to say, that the Blackbird, Goldfinch, Greenfinch and Starling are at last recognised with the Sparrow and Minah as the nuisances they undoubtedly are. It does not need the eye of a prophet to foresee that they will be joined by the English Thrush before long. The Skylark has yet to prove its usefulness or otherwise. It seems as if this mania for acclimatising anything, so long as it does not naturally belong to Australia, has gone about far enough. The touching sentiment for the homeland that led our fathers to introduce the Sparrow and Rabbit and Fox has laid a grievous burden on the orchardists and graziers of to-day. Meanwhile the noble Wild Turkey, the graceful Egrets and the Lyre Bird are becoming extinct. Cannot the Australian Natives' Association do something here? We need more stringent enforcement of the law for the protection of our native birds, which are almost to a species beneficial; and an absolute prohibition of the importation of foreign birds, which bitter experience has taught us become pests in nine cases out of ten in this country, whatever they may have been in their domicil of origin.

A curious plant, a native of Mexico, was exhibited to the club on October 3rd by the Rev. Williams, F.M.S. The name is *Selaginella convoluta*, and the specimen in Mr. Williams' possession was brought to Victoria several years ago. When the plant is in a dry state the fronds are brown in hue and incurved towards the centre, but on being placed in water it gradually opens out into a flat circle, with a diameter of about 9 inches, while the colour changes to green. After removal from the water it gradually dries up and resumes its original nest-like appearance.

The Hon. Secretary desires to acknowledge the receipt of the "Victorian Naturalist" for October and November, and the "Zoologist," Vol. VI., No. 68.

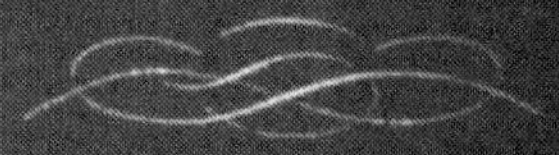

HENRY FRANKS & CO., PRINTERS, GEELONG.

www.ingramcontent.com/pod-product-compliance
Lightning Source LLC
Chambersburg PA
CBHW061101050726
47592CB00004B/1779